Taste My Soul

A Poetic Memoir

By

Monica Marie Jones

*Nikki!
Get ready to be fed with my writing too! :)*

TASTE MY SOUL. Copyright ©2007 by Monica Marie Jones. All rights reserved. Published in the United States of America. No part of this book may be used or reproduced in any manner whatsoever without written permission except in the case of brief quotations embodied in critical articles or reviews. For more information or to book the author for speaking engagements or book club appearances address The Literary Loft at Theliteraryloft@gmaill.com.

Author Information:

Monica Marie Jones

www.monicamariejones.com

monicamjones@hotmail.com

Published By:

The Literary Loft

Theliteraryloft@gmail.com

ISBN: 978-0-6151-8569-9

TABLE OF CONTENTS

INTRODUCTION **5**

TASTE MY SOUL 7

CHAPTER 1 : GRACE **11**

INSPIRATIONAL POETRY
A POOR GIRL'S PRAYER 13
ALL THAT IS LOVE 15
FAT GIRL 17
WORLD CHANGERS 21
UNCONDITIONAL 23

CHAPTER 2 : APPETIZER **25**

GENERAL POETRY
PICTORY 27
TEARS 28
NATURAL ATTACHMENT 29
TIGER EYES 30

CHAPTER 3: THE MAIN COURSE **35**

INTENSE POETRY
STEAMY SHOWERS 37
MENTAL STIMULATION 41
CONSENSUAL RAPE 44
DAMAGED GOODS 46

CHAPTER 4: AFTER DINNER DRINKS **49**

RACY POETRY
I CAME WITH HIM 51
LUST AFFAIR 54
HOT KISSES 56

CHAPTER 5: DESSERT **59**

EROTIC POETRY
LEVELS OF CHEMISTRY 61
FANTASY 66

Introduction

I am a *Fat Girl* who feels like *Damaged Goods*, that's caught up in a *Lust Affair* while striving to be a *World Changer*. The italicized phrases in the previous sentence are just a few of the titles of poems in this book that will tell you the story of me. These life experiences contribute to why I began writing when I was still holding a pencil with a small, tightly clenched fist like it was a microphone through which I spit my words with the world as my audience.

Taste My Soul is set up as a full, five course meal because it satisfies all of the senses. Once you turn this page you will dip your sensory spoon into a savory soup filled with poetry, sprinkled with a pinch of prose accompanied by a side dish of imagery that will take you on a mental expedition into the depths of my soul.

Just as with any meal it begins with *Grace* which is an assembly of inspirational poetry. *Appetizer* offers a taste of general poems that serve the purpose of whetting the appetite before digging into the good stuff. *The Main Course* is filled with intense poems that address issues such as body image, mental health, and relationships. *After Dinner Drinks* is comprised of racy poems that are spiked with suggestiveness and scandal. Last but not least, *Dessert* delves into erotic poetry. Upon completion of this book you will be affected spiritually, emotionally physically and intellectually.

Bon Appétit!

Taste My Soul

Taste My Soul one bite at a time

Or you will get full in your heart and your mind

Starved for stimulation causing strain

Gratify your desire to feed the need to end your hunger pain

Poetic gluttony takes hold of me and I regurgitate my inner being

Now my soul is bared for all to see with bits and pieces of what's inside of me

It is a full course meal

A heaping helping of what's real

Served in healthy portion sizes

It feels like no one's plate is as full as mine is

Begin with *Grace* to give thanks for what you are about to feel

The brain food that you are about to receive

A spiritual smorgasbord saturated with substance that will make you believe

The Appetizer starts with alphabet soup

Letters forming words to make lines that speak truth

Perhaps a tossed salad made with sonnet, haiku, couplet and ballad

The Main Course is a taste of soul food to stimulate your senses of sight, sound and smell

That touches your heart deeply within where it dwells

Providing sustenance and nourishment with rhythm and with rhyme

It's a gourmet delicacy so adjustment may take time

Savor the flavor of the tenderized meat

Which is the content of the poetic feast that you are preparing to eat

Take in the texture; let your taste buds go wild

Experience all levels; hot, medium and mild

Sweet soliloquy, delicious scenery and scrumptious dialogue

Salty similes, bitter analogies, tart terms thick like egg nog

Palatable poetry blended with a pinch of prose

Vitamin enriched verse given in a recommended dose

Left feeling satiated from words

Appetite has been curbed

Hard *After Dinner Drinks* go down smooth

Soaking satisfaction with every printed move

Intoxicating imagery under the influence of liquid lyrics
Drunk from shots of stanza, epic, elegy and limerick

It all ends with *Dessert*...hot, sweet and syrupy
So good you can't help but want to touch
Dripping with temptation, sensuality and lust

You will be left satiated, supplicated, satisfied and full
Stuffed to capacity...well fed... with my writing tool.

CHAPTER ONE

Grace

A Poor Girl's Prayer

Dear Lord I thank you for this day
I pray that all of my pain and struggle will go way

I pray that you will bless my friends and family
And while you're at it Lord, please bless me

I pray and ask that you will forgive me for all of my sins
For only you can cleanse me from within

I pray for those who are less fortunate than me
Please bless them (and me) financially

I pray and ask that you will lead me and guide me in your ways
Please redirect my path when I stray

You are a miracle worker indeed
I will live by your word and your word I will heed

I pray that you give me the strength to be strong
I pray that the heat will get cut back on

I thank you for all that you have done for me

Not judging me but loving me unconditionally

I pray that you will take any sickness, illness or disease out of my body right now

Thank you for teaching me tolerance, forgiveness, and devotion by showing me how

I pray that you'll increase my faith

I pray that you'll rid my heart of hate

I know that you are humbling me by testing me with poverty

I know that you are strengthening me by teaching me humility

I know that there are plenty of ways out here for me to make money

But I will wait patiently

And faithfully

Because I know you have a plan for me

Daily I'm faced with temptation, sorrow, stress and dismay

I pray that tomorrow will be a better day

Lord, until we speak again,

Know that I love you so much,

Good night

Amen

All that is Love

You brought me closer to all that is love

You discovered parts of me that were waiting to be uncovered

You are the last puzzle piece to complete all of the years of work of all that is me

You brought me closer to all that is love

You brought me closer to my spirituality

Thus bringing me closer to me

I knew myself well, but not well enough to love another

You brought the last few lessons that were needed

To complete my education of self-realization

You brought me closer to all that is love

You taught me that I do deserve good things

Yet still my faith wavered because...

"Don't all good things come to an end?"

I asked the Lord that if you were the one that *He* sent, to give me a sign

Do I really deserve this?

Could you really be mine?

You brought me closer to all that is love

Days later we sat and wrote our resolutions for the year to come

I remember your resolution number one...

"Be faithful to all that I Love."

I thought you meant me

Or your family

But how could I be so selfish?

There could be no you or no me or no family without all that you love

For all that you love is all that is love

And all that is love is the Lord

You brought me closer to all that is love

The moment I realized that this was the sign that I asked to be sent my eyes became wet

For at that moment I knew...

All that is love is the Lord

All that I love is in you

Fat Girl

A fat girl lives on the inside of me
Although I've shed the pounds I'm still weighed down
By insecurity

Mannerisms are meek and mild
Characteristics of my inner fat child

The scale and the mirror are my two biggest enemies
The scale measures failure and the mirror deceives

I don't see what others see 'cause
99% of losing weight is psychology

It has been a challenge physically
But is has been more taxing emotionally
Confusion, stress and strain afflict my psyche constantly

Put the pounds on
Now the weights gone
My life has become an oxymoron

When I was large I was invisible

Now that I'm small I cannot hide

At size 16 when it came to men, I was virtually unknown

At size 6 when it comes to men, then won't leave me alone

I can't help but wonder, would they acknowledge me the way I used to be?

For the majority, attraction is based solely on what they see

Fat jokes told in my presence offend me and confuse me even more

Then I realize, they're not meant for me, but for those who look how I looked before

Why is it then that they cut deep and still affect me so?

Because the fat child housed within refuses to let go

When I shop through the aisles and look at small clothes

My inner fat child screams, "Leave those alone!"

When I try on those clothes

I cannot believe

How the all fit me with elegance and ease

When I meet a new man that I catch feelings for

My inner fat child says,

"When he finds out that you were fat he'll head straight for the door."

With reluctance I reveal my past to that man

Using pictures as evidence of my wide waist and hip span

I prepare for him to leave as she said that he would

When he surprises me by saying, "Girl, you still used to look good!"

"Don't believe him. He's just saying that now. If he saw you back then he would call you a cow!" My inner fat child says with fury and spite putting an immediate damper on my feelings that night.

My past and my present are in a constant tug-of-war

Making it hard to appreciate all that I've worked so hard for

My will was strong but I could never win

Unless I confronted my demon within

I said "Fat girl, would you please just let me be? Just let me enjoy my new healthy body."

She said "Girl don't forget that you used to be fat. You drop a few pounds now you think you're all that? Just as you lost it you can gain it all back!"

I said "I'll never forget what I used to be. I've only changed externally. Who I am inside is the same and will always be. Now one thing is a fact, I won't gain it all back. I'm committed to keeping my lifestyle on track."

She said, "You say that now, you gluttonous sow, but I'll be here laughing when you finally back down."

I said, "I know that you thrive on my fear and self doubt, I've conquered those things so now you can get out. Your nourishment comes from my insecurity, now I am secure, so you can just leave. You used to control everything that I'd do; now I'm in control so I rebuke you!"

I was prepared for her response filled with vengeance and rage

After listening closely…

Silence was all that I could gauge

Then suddenly I heard a surrendering sigh

That escalated into a defeated child's cry

Those cries and small footsteps began to slowly fade away

I never heard from my inner fat child again after that day

World Changer

We are all going to die

So if I'm going to die

I am going to leave something for people to remember me by

Life is too short to sit and whine, complain and cry

Negativity is easy

The real challenge is to maintain and radiate positive energy

I know that I was placed on this Earth to do great things globally

I wait patiently and humbly as these things are revealed to me

Every day HE humbles me with tests like poverty and folks who talk about me

So that when the blessings come I'll have humility and a testimony

I better get all of the sleep I can now

Because when I'm assigned to my destiny there will be no time to lie down

I can sleep when I'm dead

Besides, peace and silence never come when I sleep

Thoughts and ideas pollinate my mind like bees

I've got to sleep with paper and pen next to me

To record all of the visions that I see

Which I plan to convert to reality

It will be interesting to see which path will be chosen for me

Will it be writing, politics or the entertainment industry?

Speaking engagements or ministry?

Or all of the above?

For these are all things that I love

I don't just want to make a difference

I want to change the world

Like the man who had a dream for little white and black boys and girls

When I am dead I won't really die

Because the legacy I leave will keep me alive

Unconditional

I've always felt the need to run away

Before I met you, I never had a reason that made me want to stay

Now that you are here my life is all in disarray

But in a good way...

When I'm without you, every minute seems like a day

But when I'm with you time just seems to fly away

I will be with you, forever...

A promise so sincere

As I prepare to sleep alone I know that rest will not find me without you here

Just the mere thought that you are near...

Close enough for you to wake me by kissing away my nightmare tears

No more sadness, abandonment, betrayal or deceit

I take my life, my love, my heart and place them at your feet

A love so sincere

You'll never have to fear

A faithfulness beyond this world

Will always keep me here

CHAPTER TWO

Appetizer

Pictory

One thousand words worth of history

An in depth story in captivity

I'll never forget the day you captured me

Extracting beauty from beneath layers of insecurity

Confirming confidence and self assurance

Pictorials give testimonials to individuals solely on visuals

Warm lighting envelopes me enhancing my features so colorfully

Two dimensional artistry

Captured in various measurements...

3x5, 4x6, 5x7, 8x10

Magnificence is magnified when your eye meets the lens

Tears

Her skin and her features give the appearance of youth

But when you look deep into her eyes her soul speaks the truth

Experience and wisdom beyond her years

Spill forth from those eyes captured in tears

The tracks that are left tell the story in depth

They're the trail of the journey of a heart that has wept

Natural Attachment

I am around you frequently
So naturally
Your beauty captures me...

So how is it that naturally
I can detach from you emotionally?

My need to see you
Be with you
And feel you
Increases with great urgency
So naturally my love for you
Steadily increases too

Whatever I set out to do
I find my thoughts roam back to you

So how is it that naturally we can fight what has to be?

Attraction becomes a variable
Attachment becomes inevitable
Feelings far from what seems sensible
All else is incomprehensible

Hard to turn back
Hard not to act
Hard to fight that
Which simply is...
Emotions will not give
Any mercy...

As much as we rehearse the
Line that says that we're "just friends"

The truth is that the rule gets stretched and bends
Especially when we are holding hands

An energy passes through and connects us two
So what are we to do
But submit to "me and you"
And become "we"...

Naturally.

Tiger Eyes

The bar was straight; the club was alright,

But nothing too interesting had happened that night

And they weren't finished yet 'cause the weather was tight

At 2am Detroit shuts down

Except for the pulsating beats at Trench Town

Reggae was not what they had on their minds

A good time is what they were trying to find.

Where could they go? What could they do?

Then Mackenzie suggested, "Let's go to the stu."

"What is the stu?" Madison asked Mackenzie as she twisted her face quizzically.

"My friend has a studio out in Farmington Hills. It's really nice. We can hang out, listen to some good music and just relax. And there are always a lot of men there." Mackenzie answered with a sly smile.

"That's cool. You know I'm down for whatever," is what Madison said, but she was really thinking... *This is going to be so whack! But I am going to go and support my girl. She is obviously motivated to go because there is someone there that she is interested in. I'm really not even trying to meet any new men, especially after the lame ones we just left at the club.*

They pulled up to the building where there was a single car in an otherwise empty parking lot. Madison thought... *Great, there is only one car here, which means her friend is probably here by himself. They are going to be all cuddled up and I am going to be sitting here alone, staring at a wall. I knew I should have brought a good book to read.*

The building was unmarked. As they approached the entrance, a male figure darkened the doorway. Once they crossed over the threshold they were engulfed in a sea of blue walls as they walked through halls that seemed to go on forever heading to who knows where, what, or whom... A figure emerged from the darkness. *At least there's on other guy here,* Madison thought to herself.

The air smelled thick like the sweat excreted from the pores of the skin of men hard at work, concentrating, creating...it was almost intimidating. They stepped into a cozy room with a level of comfort that was a complete contrast to the emptiness of the halls and rooms that came before it. The mood was somber and the room's inhabitants were just within the reach of slumber's grasp...

When the ladies emerged, sleepiness turned to silliness, laziness became laughter, all manifested through small talk and chatter. The air was thick and heavy, bogged down with the nervous energy and tension that is ever present during first encounters. Mackenzie's words were the knife that cut the cloud of thickness that loomed over the room, the pick that broke the ice. "Hello everyone, this is Madison, Madison, this is everyone." Madison responded by saying a chipper, yet coy, "Hello everyone." She then took a step forward so that she could be in clear view of everyone in the room, visually taking in all, but making eye contact with none, until **_HE_** opened his eyes...

Eyes meet

Eyes lock

She shifts in her seat

He looks at the clock

Oooh look at his eyes

Mmmmm look at her thighs

The magnetism is so instant and powerful

That it catches them both off guard

She's feeling wet

He's feeling hard

They are feeling' each other in more ways than one

The allure between them has already begun

Everyone was in the room

But it felt like no one at all

Except for HE and SHE who were beginning to fall...

"What size shoe do you wear?" asks some random guy in the room, snapping Madison back to reality.

"Huh...what?" She asks puzzled.

"You said that your feet hurt, do you want me to rub them for you?" He asks sincerely. "No I'm straight." She answered, but the truth was that she wasn't straight at all. She

had been shaken to the core by the sensual energy she felt pass between her and the man with the tiger eyes. His eyes intrigued her, they were shaped like almonds, and they were fixed on her. She turned all of her attention back to him. They shared small talk but she wanted more, and he wanted more.

"Why don't you walk me to the car?" She asked shyly. Being forward was new to her but she was no stranger to knowing what she wanted and going after what she wanted, and what she wanted was him. They walked out into the warm night air, hand in hand. Positive energy flowed through their connection, making them one...

They were...

Diggin' and vibin' and feelin'and smilin'

Analyzin' and philosophizin' and just plain old wilin' out

So much to talk about

But time did not belong to them alone,

'Cause she had someone waiting at home

And he is also with another

The chemistry must be kept under cover

But the attraction has caused a chemical reaction

Building up

Boiling over

About to explode...

"When can I see you again?" He asked regretting that the evening had to come to a close.

"I'm not sure, but I am going to try my best to make it sooner than you think." She answered wishing that the night did not have to end.

They went their separate ways. During the long drive home she replayed the night over and over in her head inserting bits of fantasy within the reality of what went down that night. He intrigued her; there was just something about his entire being that touched her on the inside. How can you fight a feeling so strong? Attraction... Desire... Magnetism... Allure...Fascination...Enthrallment...

Wishing, Wanting, Yearning, Craving...
The man with the Tiger Eyes.

CHAPTER THREE

The Main Course

Steamy Showers

Although that night was intense, time had begun to erode the vivid pictures of pleasure that were once fresh in their minds. Against their will they were forced to exit their worlds of real fantasy and thrown back into the complicated routines of their everyday realities.

As she carried on throughout her weekly responsibilities her mind would occasionally drift to him, him with her, him with her that night...

His schedule was so demanding that his mind barely had time to wander. One night he was taking a shower to unwind from the day's events when his mind glided to thoughts of her. The hot liquid engulfed his body and caused some severe flashbacks. It reminded him of how it felt to be inside of her, so hot, so wet. As the water continued to envelope his body it reminded him of how she wrapped her solid thighs around his waist and back, a welcome supplementation to the sensation of the penetration, so hot, so wet...

That same night she lay in her bed fantasizing about him taking a shower. She pictured the individual droplets of water rolling down all 2000 parts of his enticing physique. She fixated her focus onto one drop in particular. When it left the showerhead it landed on the top of his head. It rolled down his forehead to the bridge of his nose where it veered right and grazed the corner of those sexy tiger eyes. It proceeded to follow the crease of his smile where it made a sharp left and tumbled over one soft lip after another...over the curve of his chin, it then trickled slowly down the center of his neck, then picked up speed between his collarbones where it curved to the right near his pectoral muscles and outlined the tiger that he had tattooed there.

It went over his nipple then down to his stomach where it made a left at his abs and went in and then out of his navel. It navigated its way through the pubic area to a place so smooth, yet so hard. It started at the base then it traveled and traveled and traveled and traveled and traveled and traveled and traveled until it FINALLY reached the tip....

She was suddenly jarred from her fantasy by the loud crackle of thunder. She was slightly dampened by a thin mist of sweat caused by the humidity in the air and the power of the flight of the imagination. She stepped out onto the patio and watched the lightning line the night sky...

The air was thick like her soft supple thighs

The scent was sexy like his almond shaped eyes

The pavement was hot like her throbbing G spot

Ribbons of lightning illuminated the night sky

You could smell the rain coming, though the streets were still dry

The night was dark like the room where they lay

Thunder cried out like the moans of foreplay

For a moment there was silence and there was nothing else in the world but the two of them... the earth; waiting, needing, wanting, for the rain to cum. The rain; waiting, needing, wanting to be one with the earth...

The raindrops came down, long, and hard and penetrated the earth with thrusts so deep that they were felt at the core

The earth shuddered with pleasure for being given what it had been waiting for

The drops titillated the treetops and saturated the soft spots

The rain and the earth were one

A physical bond had begun

The rain had cum...

The raindrops had cooled and the pavement was hot causing steam to rise after they had both stopped...

They thought that since the rain had stopped and the earth had spilled forth with an abundance of satisfaction that it was all done and over with, but it was only the beginning of something more deep, more extreme. The earth wanted more rain and the rain wanted to become one with the earth again. They *needed* one another; want was no longer an option. But all that they could do was wait patiently, until it was time, but this time, they would go all night...

Mental Stimulation

When I left your house I parked on a cloud and floated home

I keep replaying thoughts of you with me in my mind

So vivid it's hard to believe that I'm alone

'Cause I'm feelin' high from being with you and it's got me so gone

Keep licking my lips to taste the remnants of your kiss

Got me hot, not from stimulating my g spot

Got me hot not from ripping off my pants and my top

Got me wet, not from kissin' on my neck

Got me wet, not from what we might expect

Got me hot, got me wet, from an intellectual train wreck

Turned on by your train of thought

When it crashed into my train causing wreckage in the brain

The impact so intense you got me bent

The collision so abrupt you got me...

Messed up

Fiery foreplay in the form of conversation, libation and sharing of our poetry

We had to find a way to channel that electric energy

So that we would not combust spontaneously

So naturally we squelched that fire physically

Words are what bonded us but our bond is beyond words

So we sealed our bond with a kiss

To confirm our mutual experience of pure bliss

Yellow caution tape wrapped round our fate

Because it is so rare to meet someone to whom you can relate

And so dangerous that two minds

Can be so powerfully intertwined

That they cross the lines

Of reason and of rhyme

And trigger the physical side

Mental stimulation got me hot and wet

And ready to get more of what is yet to come

A special connection has begun

Beware of the power of the potential when two great minds become one

Consensual Rape

He liked her, but she really wasn't feelin' him no more
Despite the fact that they'd had sex before

He turned her off with his conniving ways
He would have said or done anything just to make her stay

He got her good and drunk that night
To make sure that she wouldn't put up a fight

He didn't "git it" or "hit it"
He took it from behind

While she was drunk and passed out
No consent came from her mouth

The irritating friction caused when rubber meets dry flesh
Was the thing that woke her up to find herself undressed

Before she could protest the act was already in progress
Rather than putting up a fight, she chose instead to digress

Besides, it was her conscious choice to drink beyond her limit

But it was her birthday, so didn't she deserve it

Yeah it was true that they kicked it now and then
But she still had the right to say if and when
She wanted to have sex with him again

If it had been her choice she would have chosen not to
Inebriation impaired her ability to choose
When you are under the influence good judgment is the first thing that you lose

But how could she choose to object or concede
When all of this took place while she was fast asleep

He took advantage of her vulnerability
Ravaged her body inconspicuously

The thought of what took place caused her heart to ache
He was someone she knew, they were out on a date

It tormented her to know that she contributed to her fate
So she silently gave in to Consensual Rape

Damaged Goods

Outer beauty covers her torture within

Her eyes tell the story of her shame for her sins

She's unaware of the attractiveness that she emits
In her eyes the mirror reflects her internal anguish

Daylight illuminates her vibrant smile and infectious personality
Night fall hides her silent cries and tears that fall when no one else can see

Each day she adds a brick to the wall that she has built
To keep the pain out and conceal all the guilt

She uses destructive behaviors to deal
Sex, greed and gluttony forbid her to feel

Promiscuity masks her insecurity

Alcohol leads to her downfall

They help her escape from a world filled with hate
Where innocence is kidnapped by abandonment and rape
And love is side swept by abuse and neglect

No father figure to intercept her love

So her love is transferred to bad boys and thugs

She'll do anything in her power to keep who she has

For fear that they might up and leave her like dad

The ones that truly care, she pushes away

Because maybe, they too, will leave her some day

No motivation to live her life as she knows that she should

Because who in their right mind would accept, want, cherish or love…

Damaged Goods

CHAPTER FOUR

After Dinner Drinks

I Came With Him

I came with him...then I met you...

Caught you staring at me from across the room...

I soon realize that averting my eyes becomes harder than ever...

An undeniable gravitational pull forces us together...

I was captured by your captivating conversation...

Captivating conversation transforms into flirtation...

Vibrating vocal chords voicing verbal stimulation

All thoughts of what is right fly by quickly with the time...

Like the fact that we both realize that our intentions are out of line...

I came here with him...but now I'm feelin' you...

Our connection is so strong it feels like we're the only ones in the room...

Eventually everyone went their separate ways....

Those gravitational forces then pulled you to my place...

We made an honest attempt to discuss and rationalize the situation at hand...

But that is when the physical connection began...

We began to bask in the bliss of the bond between our bodies…

The instant your lips touched my lips was the moment that you got me…

Nothing mattered anymore once our bodies met the floor…

Me on top of you ready and eager to explore…

Articles of clothing come off with haste…

Our need for one another is urgent, no time to waste…

Fragrance and illumination of scented candles penetrate the room….

Initial penetration so deep it infiltrates the womb…

Pleasurable pressure fills me up so thick that every wall within is hit…

My wet walls wrapped around you so tight

There's no doubt we'll both cum tonight

Climactical reactions

Confirm utter satisfaction

As we engage in this action

Of our mutual attraction

That we can't possibly deny

Or we would both be telling lies

Now all we can do is try

To resist a second time

Of our bodies intertwined

As I slow wind and slow grind

While you hit it from behind

Scenes keep replaying in my mind...

I came with him...you made me cum...

How could something so wrong be so much fun?

Lust Affair

Moist between the thighs from gazing into those sexy eyes

Heart racin' at the smell of Sweet Temptations

Talkin, toucin', teasin' tastin',

So sweet, so sexy, so soft, so sensual,

So special, so sumptuous, so sincere, so sexual ...

Shuddering, sweating, shivering, shaking

Satisfaction, supplication, supplementation, sensation

You got me using alliteration to exemplify the titillation

Can't stop staring at you

Trying to take it all in

Enough to last me until we meet again

Don't want to leave you but I have to go home

Mind so stuck on you I can't concentrate on the road

Legs still quivering got me swerving and swaying

Crossing over the mid line praying

That I make it home safely

I reminisce on how you taste me

Heart still beating fast

How long will this feeling last?

Head straight for the tub so he won't smell you on me

You do the same, wash my essence down the drain

So that she won't smell me and know that you came… without her

And I came without him, repercussions would be grim

If he or she found out that we let this lust affair begin

And lust affair it is 'cause you love her and I love him

Emotions become an oxymoron as I am taken away by Calgon

Glad… 'Cause this steamy shower feels so good

Mad… 'Cause the erotic essence of you that is emanating from me

Is being washed down the drain so instantly…

Hot Kisses

Grey Goose had him feelin' loose

The Chardonnay began to make her sway

He saw her from behind

She saw him take the stage

Strong Features

Her lashes, lips and legs

His bald head, russet skin and slow blink that revealed his sexy gaze

Her lips, full and glossy, parted slightly

Inviting what might be…

Two models

Both fine

Had everyone looking their way

Envious stares from admirers and suitors

Glares from guys who wanted to be him so that they could be closer to her...

Looks from ladies that wanted to be her so that they could be closer to him...

Proximity between the two is getting really thin
She opens her mouth to speak when he stops her by grabbing her chin
Words meant to escape her mouth were pushed back down by his tongue
The room filled with people became a room filled with none...

But those two...
Bound together like glue...

Joined at the lips...
Unable to break loose...

CHAPTER FIVE

DESSERT

Levels of Chemistry

She scans him

He scans her

Conversation filled with humor is exchanged to mask the nervousness that occurs

The chemistry between a man and a woman gives birth to mutual attraction

They are intrigued by the mere presence of one another

They acknowledge their feelings and move on with their lives

Leaving that clear connection behind

Because neither can act on what they are feeling

So they try their best not to be revealing

He is "involved" and she is "involved" but neither can deny that which has evolved

The magnetism should signify that "Its 'bout to be on"

The problem is that the timing is all wrong

The setting was wrong as well

The scene was professional

So they touched each other on an intellectual level

The only touching that was acceptable

For now, that would have to suffice

Because how they really wanted to touch each other was not quite as nice...

The setting was wrong and the timing was wrong...

But the FEELING was all right

Time passes and feelings are placed to the side

But as more time passes they get harder to hide...

The scenery changes to a more social setting

It's nighttime

Drinking

Dancing

Sweet talking

Romancing

The air is hot like the steam that rises from the undulating bodies intertwined that grind to the pulsating beat of the bass, ready and willing to get just a taste...

Of each other

Feelings can no longer be covered

He was feelin' her dancing when he peeped her thong

Dang

Didn't she know that those things turned him on?

It had shown just above her tight low rise jeans

Which got his mind to racing and wandering and thinking about things...

She feels a bulge between his legs, above the knees

That's growing and stretching and trying to break free...

But he's not the only one that's aroused

Because she is so wet that her panties are doused...

They are closer than close

But not close enough

Until they connect like a hand fits in glove...

They touch each other on a physical level...

It is what it is and it can't be denied

When attraction is there it's just too hard to hide

A look or a touch or a sigh or a stare

Or an intimate thought when there's nobody there

Exchanging text messages along the way...

"I can't stop thinking about you sexy"

    -Or-

"Dang, you sure looked nice today."

They try to forget but it won't go away...

They want each other more with each passing day

It may be infatuation

It might just be lust

But rectifying the situation is an absolute must

They need, want, have to have each other, now

It's too powerful for either of them to hold it all down

Her thick thighs quiver in anticipation of ecstasy and pure sensation

So wet, so hot, nipples like rocks, from the licking and sucking and kissing and rubbing

She fights to break free from her sexual trance and mystifies him with an exotic dance

She finishes off by massaging her clit, then licks her own juices, so hot, wet, and thick

After watching her self-pleasure he can't take it any more
His manhood is the key and her womanhood, the door

They rock back and forth in syncopated rhythm
His member is the inmate, her private place, the prison

Pure pleasure, pure bliss, she got hers, he got his…
This must be what living a fantasy is

It's over for now, they've settled the score
But it was so good it only made them want more…

Fantasy

Thursday night.

11:56pm.

Just got through watching REAL SEX

Now you're on my mind again

My burning desire for you manifests itself in the form of hot wetness

Flowing down the canal within

The journey was so slow, so long, saturating my red lace thong

I tried to hold it back

I tried to be your good girl

I squeezed my thighs together tight

But that just made it feel all the more right

My finger cyclically massages my clit

Dang! I can't believe you've got me doing all this

I close my eyes tight

The back of my eyelids become motion picture screens

You are the leading man of the film that I see

Camera zooms in on your eyes then zooms out to capture your sexy body

I enter stage left

Wrap my thighs around your neck

What I thought was my finger becomes your tongue

You whisper, "Baby, I want to make you cum."

I want to please you as much as you please me

I stand up

Push you against the wall

And drop to my knees

My saliva is hot

I use it to saturate my tongue and wet my lips

I start at your left inner thigh

Work my way up

And outline your hip

When I start, my tongue is the first thing to touch your skin

Then I close down with my lips to take your taste in

My mouth and my tongue and my lips got over zealous

So much so that my womanhood got jealous

It got hotter and wetter as it waited patiently

As it waited to take all of you inside of me

I crawled up your body making us face to face

We kissed hard and deep and sensuously

You tasting you

And me tasting me

I lower my pelvis down onto you slow

As we become one I am feeling you grow

I start winding and grinding and doing the hip roll

You match all of my movements

Blow for blow

Going deeper

And deeper...

I can't take it no more...

Arch my back

Head thrown back

Eyes roll back

Thick hair wet with sweat stuck to my face and my neck

Climax starts at my core and spreads through my body like the Doppler Effect

A soft yet deep moan escapes my lips above...

A liquid silk escapes my lips below

I slowly open my eyes to the bright TV glow...

You're not here...

It's just me...

In the dark...

All alone...

Acknowledgements

God. Thank you for the <u>test</u>s, so that I may minister to others through my <u>test</u>imony.

Ray, Mom and JR. Thank you for always allowing me to be me and loving me through it unconditionally.

Kalita, Renae, and Monike. Thank you for sticking by me, judgment free, while I was trying to get to know me.

MONICA MARIE JONES is the author of *The Ups and Downs of Being Round*, *Taste My Soul* and *FLOSS*. She is a contributing author in *Chicken Soup for the Girls Soul* and *New Directions for Youth Development*. She received her Bachelor's degree in Elementary Education from Eastern Michigan University and her Master's of Social Work from the University of Michigan. Currently she resides in Detroit, Michigan where she is pursuing her purpose and her passion of writing full time. To book the author for spoken word performances email theliteraryloft@gmail.com. To learn more information or to contact the author visit her website at www.monicamariejones or send an email to monicamjones@hotmail.com

Made in the USA
Charleston, SC
11 March 2010